YOUR VERY FAVORITE Cute Pets COLORING BOOK FOR KIDS!

Thanks to your purchase, we are able to donate books to kids in long-term hospital care, foster care, and homeless shelters.

HAS YOUR CHILD COLORED A MASTERPIECE? CAREFULLY CUT OUT THE PAGE AND FRAME IT OR HANG IT ON THE FRIDGE!

WANT TO PRINT MORE?
BUY THE PRINTABLE VERSION OF THIS BOOK AT CARAVANSHOPPE.COM/PRODUCTS/BOOKS-CUTEPETS

First Printing: 2021

ISBN: 978-1-7361663-7-6

Caravan Shoppe books are available at special discounts when purchased for promotions, fundraising, and educational use. Special editions or book excerpts can also be created. For details, contact hello@caravanshoppe.com.

Illustrated by Mike Loveland, with contributions by Alma Loveland and Holly Sparks.

Printed in the United States of America.

caravan

www.caravanshoppe.com

MIXED BREED DOG

RED-EARED SLIDER

SUGAR GLIDER

COCKATIEL

CHAMELEON

COMMON DEGU

HERMIT CRAB

CAT

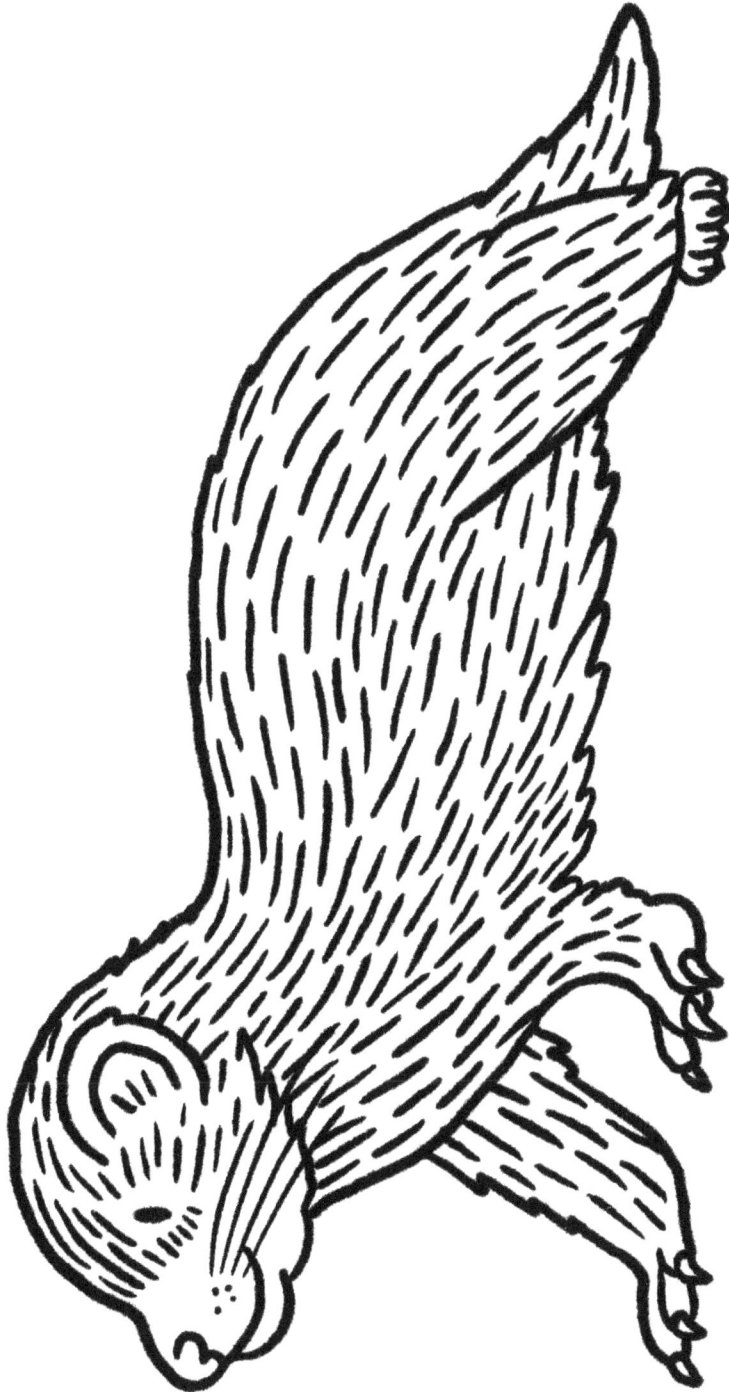

BABY FERRET

BOSTON TERRIER DOG

CAPYBARA

HAMSTER

TORTOISE

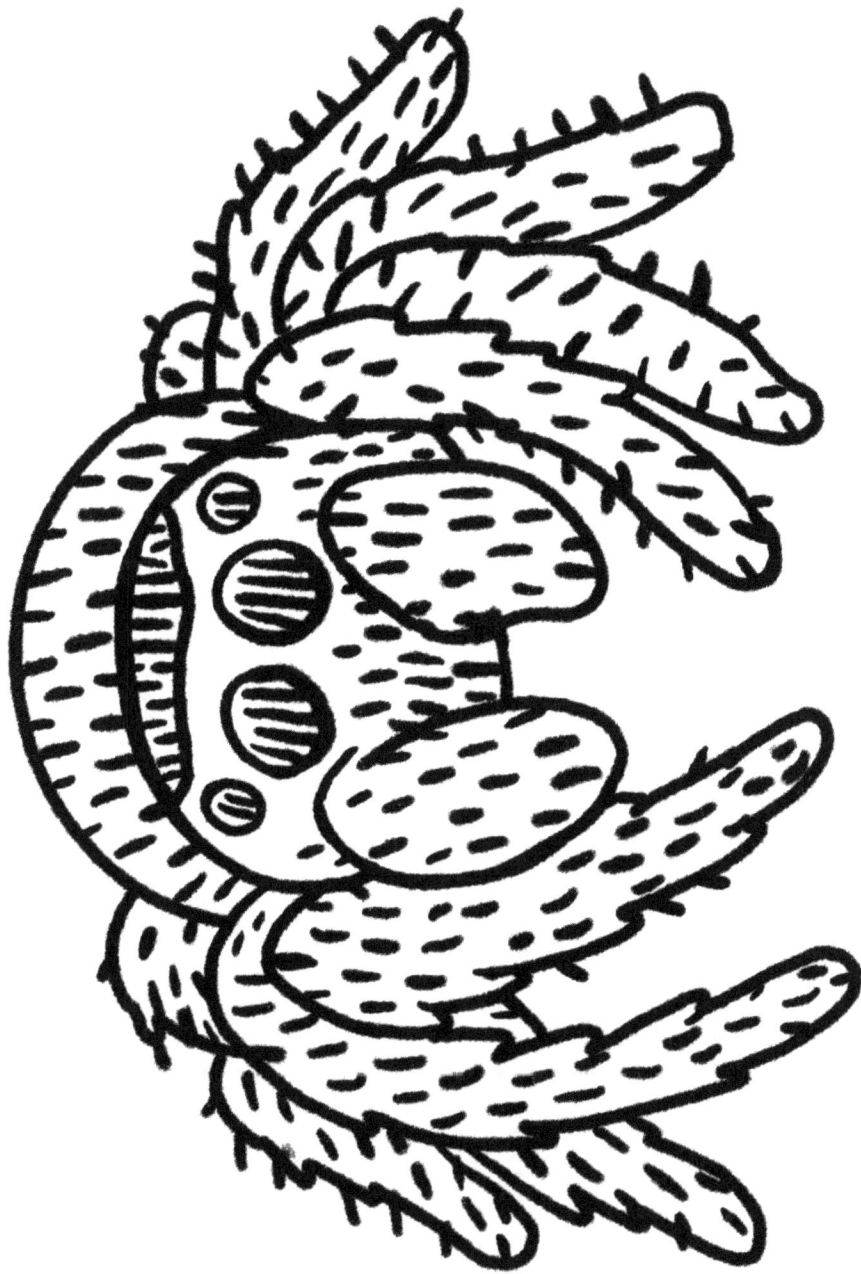

TARANTULA

COCKATOO

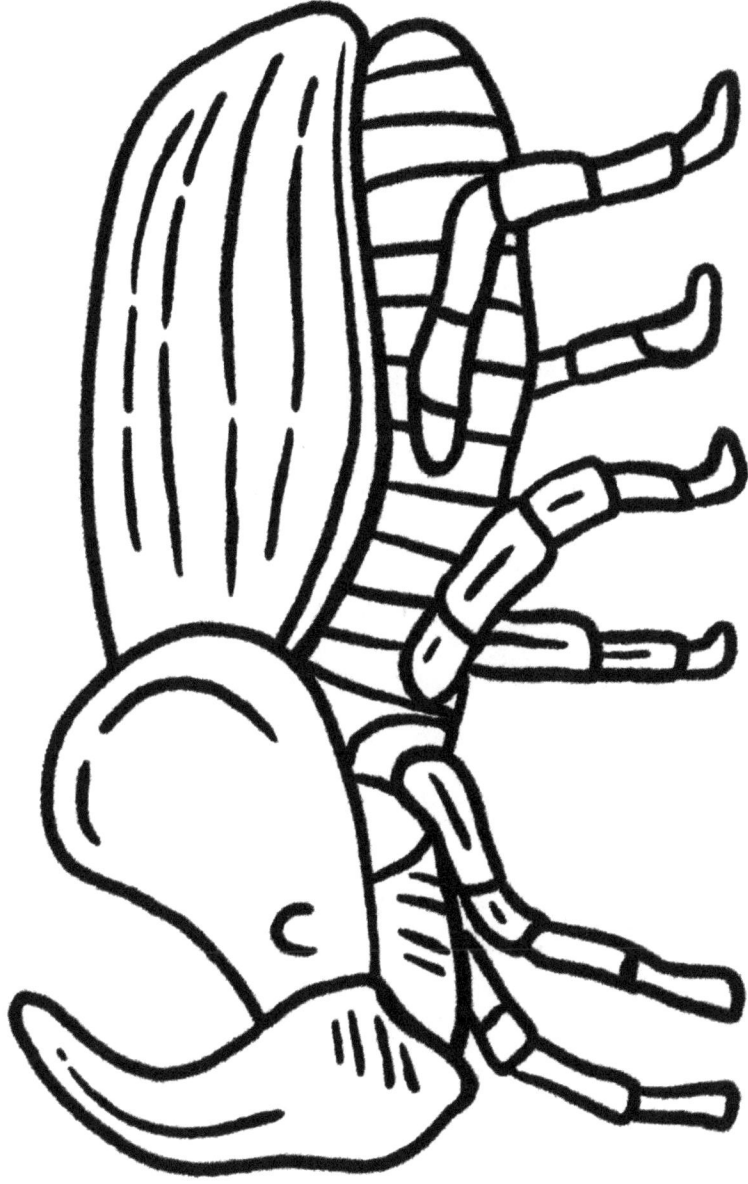

RABBIT

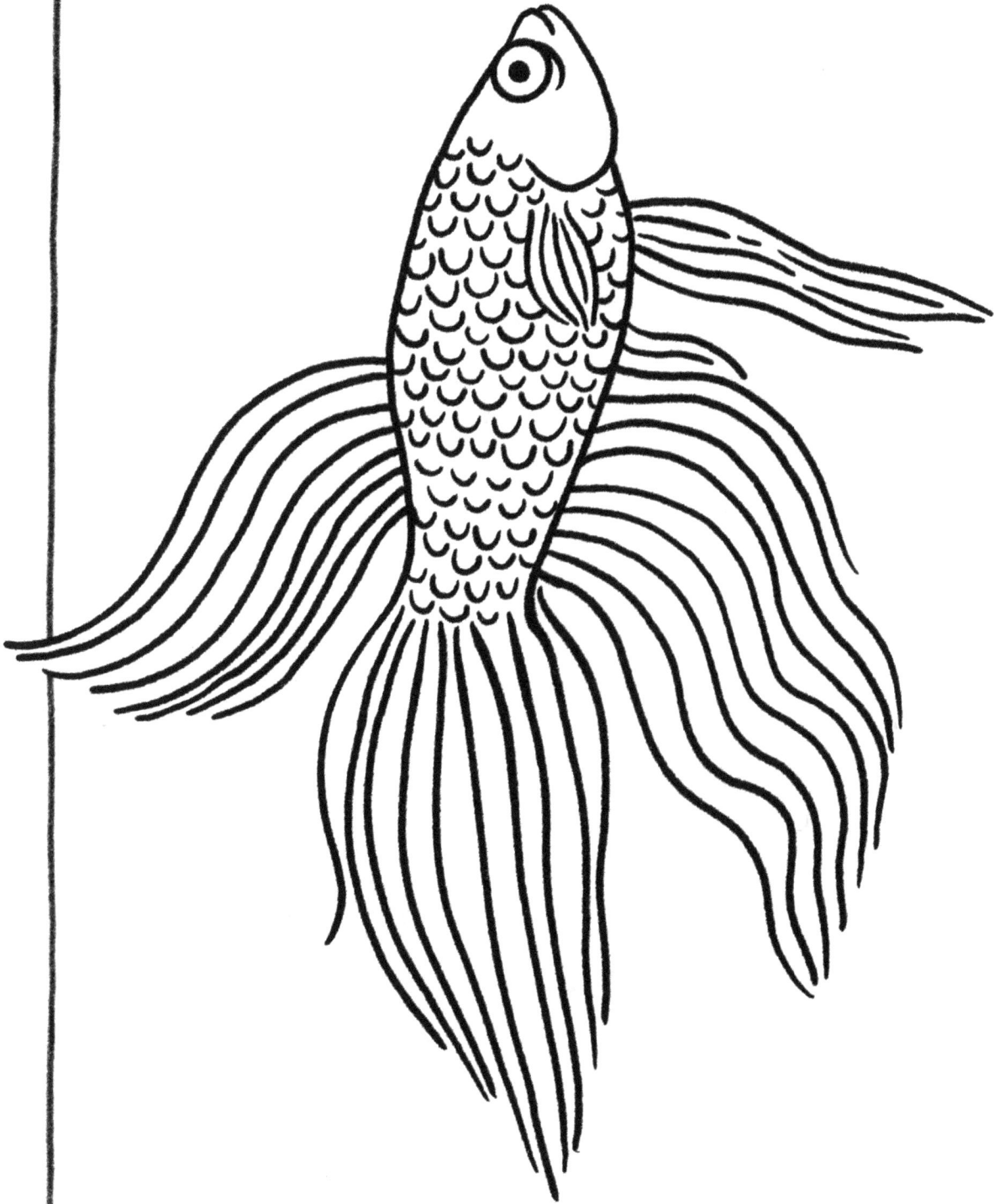

BETTA FISH

CHIHUAHUA DOG

GUINEA PIG

FINCH

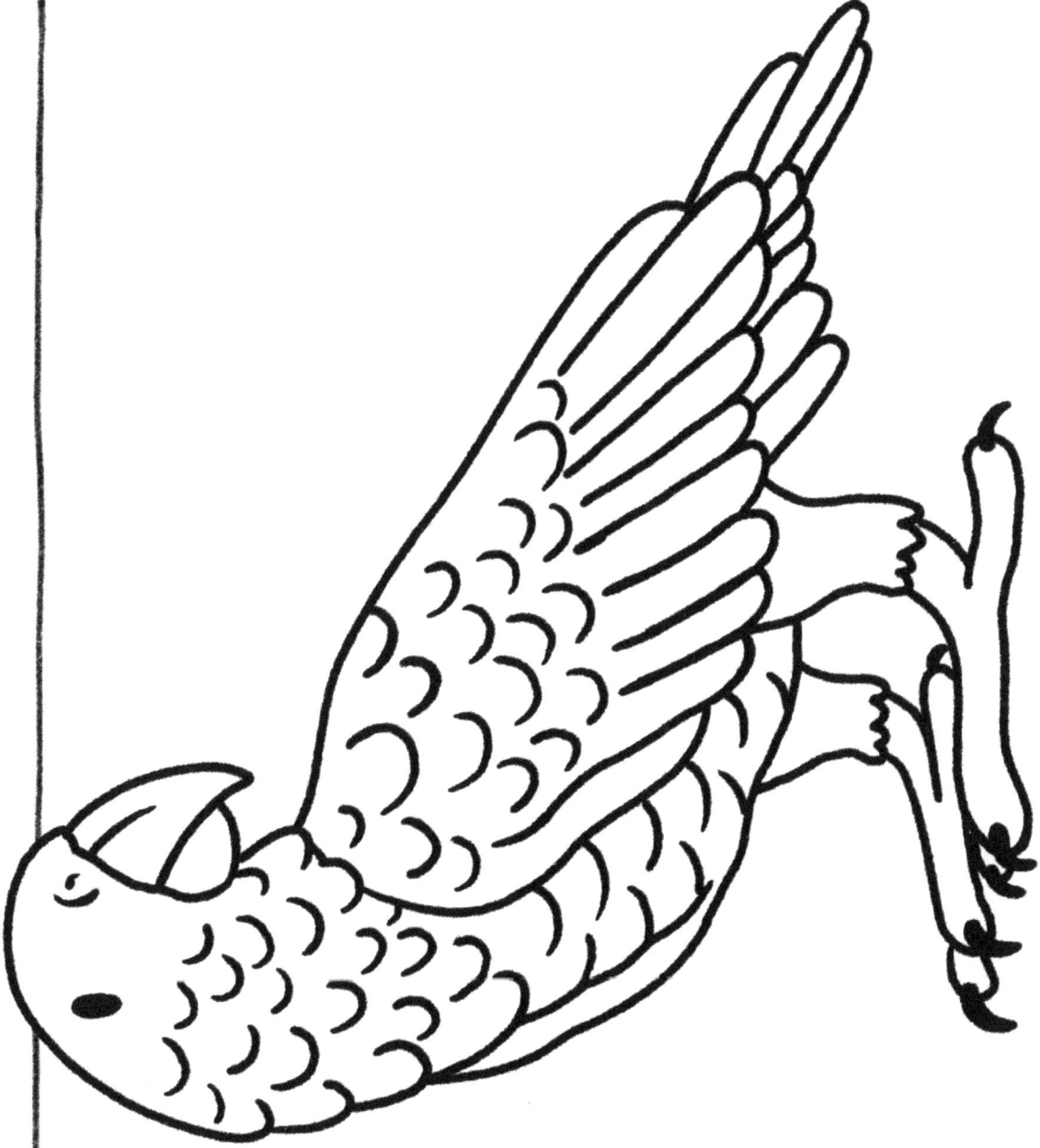

PARROT

PULI DOG

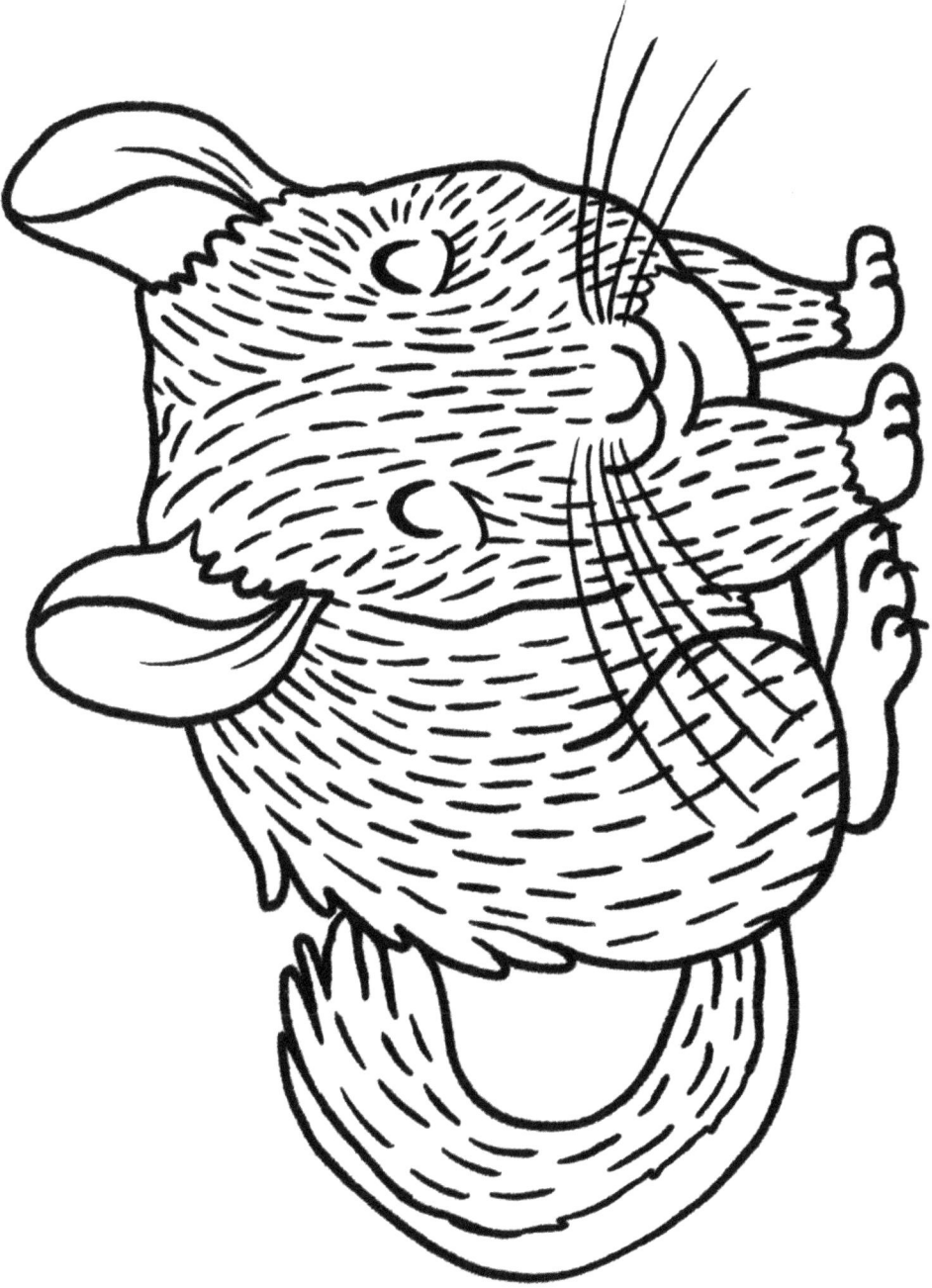

CHINCHILLA

LLAMAS

PET SNAKE

HEDGEHOG

PET FROG

GERBIL

NEWFOUNDLAND DOG

FANCY RAT

HAMSTER

LEOPARD GECKO

CAT

PARAKEET

IGUANA

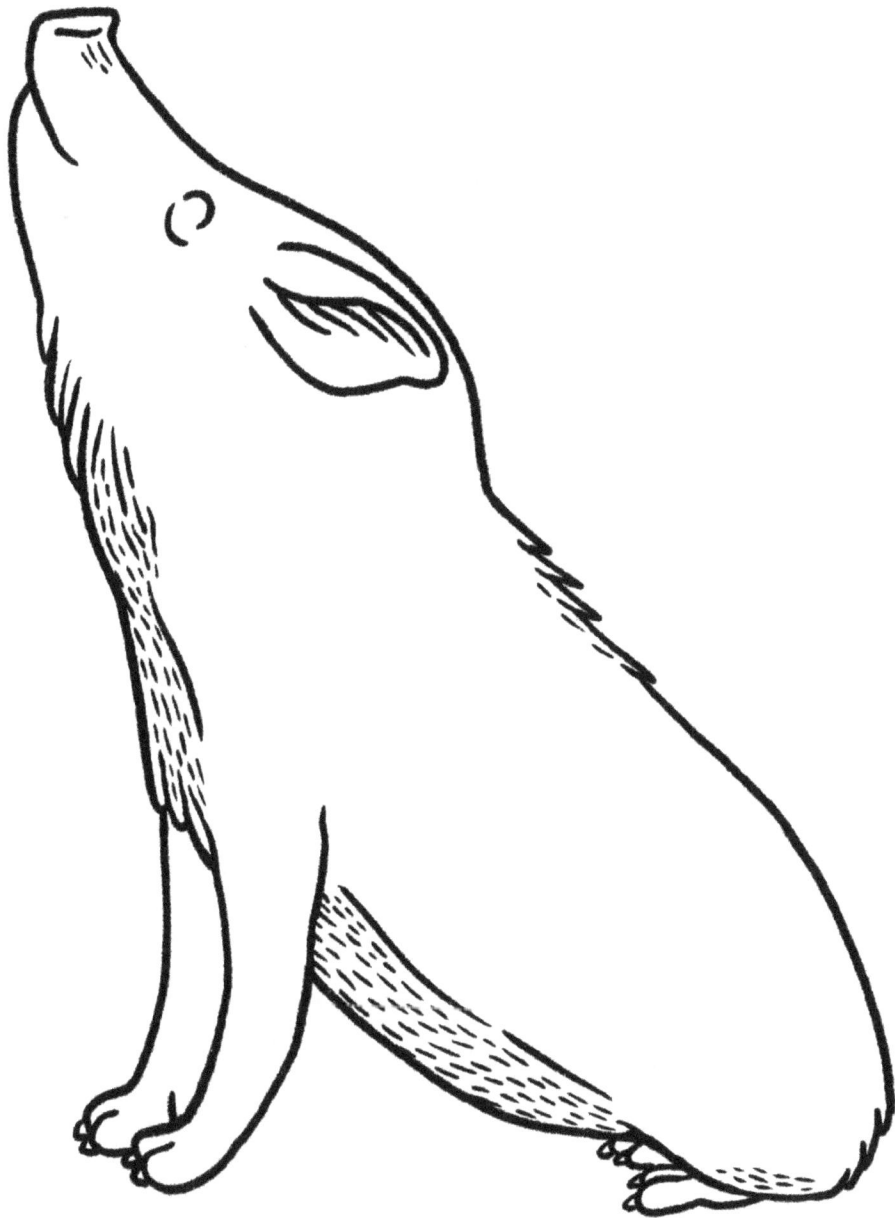

PET PIG

DO YOUR SIBLINGS AND FRIENDS WANT TO COLOR THESE PAGES, TOO?

WISH YOU COULD COLOR YOUR FAVORITE PAGE ALL OVER AGAIN?

50%OFF

GET 50% OFF A PRINTABLE VERSION OF THIS BOOK!

WE'VE GOT MORE TO COLOR!

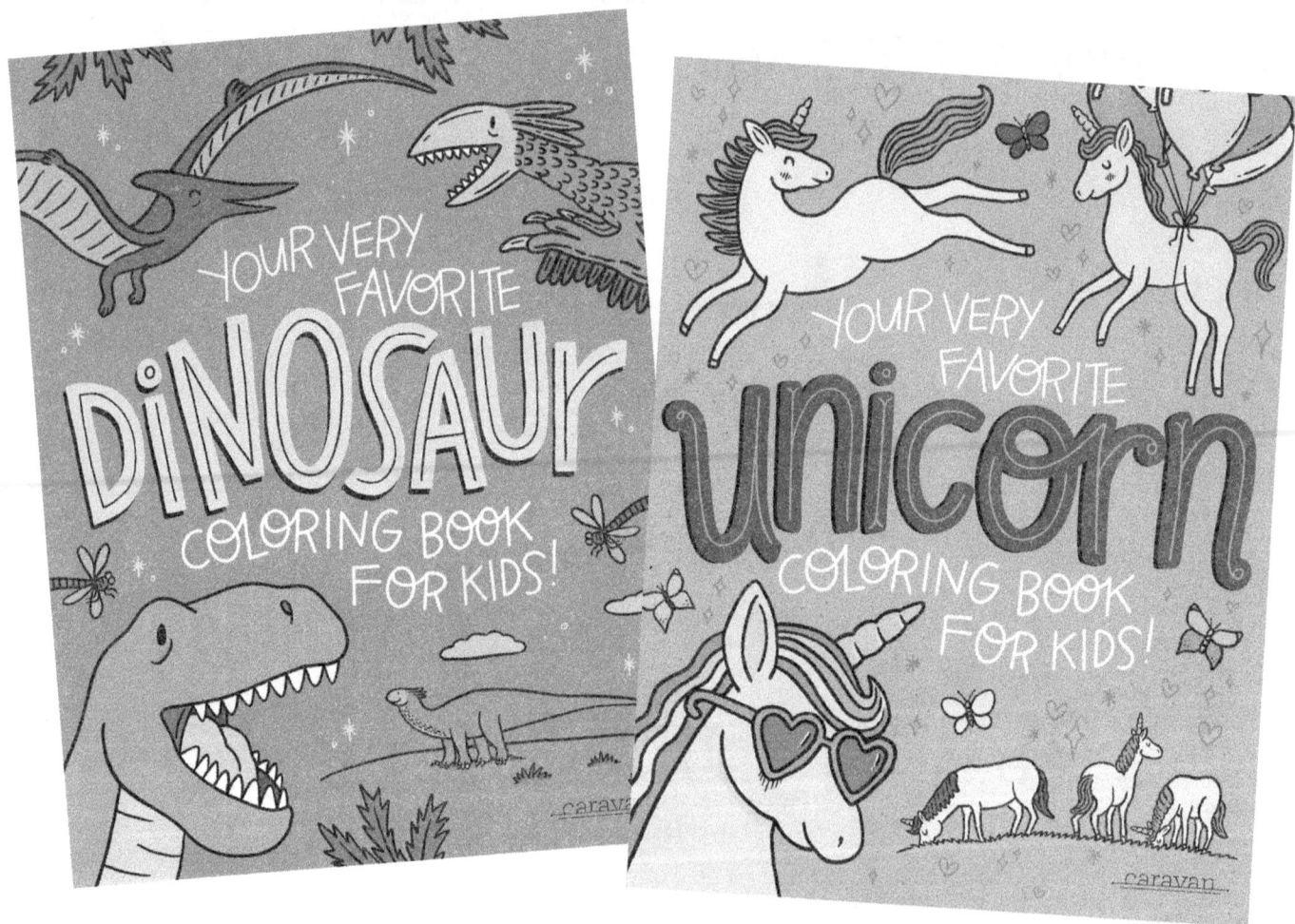

YOUR VERY FAVORITE **DiNOSAUR** COLORING BOOK FOR KIDS!

YOUR VERY FAVORITE **unicorn** COLORING BOOK FOR KIDS!

LEAVE US A REVIEW!
(AND TELL A MILLION OF YOUR FRIENDS!)

WE'RE ALREADY WORKING ON OUR NEXT BOOKS AND WE LOVE YOUR FEEDBACK AND REQUESTS! SEND US AN EMAIL AT HELLO@CARAVANSHOPPE.COM.

YOU'RE ALSO GONNA LOVE THESE ACTIVITY BOOKS!

★★★★★

This is the best activity book! My kids have gone through A LOT of activity books over the years so I speak from experience when I say that the quality of this book FAR exceeds anything else we've tried. Each activity is unique and creative and my son loved the variety. I loved hearing my 8 year old snicker to himself while doing the book. We will definitely be purchasing more!

★★★★★

This book is amazing. My kids lose interest in coloring books, so I was hesitant about purchasing this. My fantasy loving 12 year old son LOVES this book. All of it is golden, the clever sayings, cute writing and fun illustrations. The quizzes, word searches and coloring pages are all perfect for a wide range of kids. My boys are 7–14 and they have been passing it around having a great time.

WANT MORE?

SUPER
SAMPLER
BONUS
PACK

KEEP THE FUN GOING WITH
MORE TO COLOR!

SIGN UP TO RECEIVE OCCASIONAL EMAIL UPDATES,
AND WE'LL SEND YOU THIS SUPER SAMPLER BONUS
PACK OF ALL-NEW COLORING PAGES!

SCAN THIS
WITH A
SMART PHONE

OR VISIT:
https://bit.ly/3BgUuiZ

www.ingramcontent.com/pod-product-compliance
Lightning Source LLC
Chambersburg PA
CBHW080551030426
42337CB00024B/4838